AF605332

ngayawanj bagan-nggul, ngayawanj barra barra-nggul

we belong to the land, we belong to the sea

VINCENTIA HIGH SCHOOL
with Kirli Saunders and Jaz Corr

CONTENTS

INTRODUCTION

Vincentia High has been at the forefront of language revitalisation for the best part of two decades. Through strong leadership and community support Dhurga has been established as a compulsory subject that every student in Year 7 undertakes. The subject not only teaches the phonetic and grammatical aspects of language, it encourages students to view the world from an Indigenous perspective, giving them an insight into the cultural traditions and practices that have sustained the land and sea for countless millennia. Integral to this is understanding the interconnection between all elements of the natural world. The poems in this collection celebrate the relationship our students have with the land and sea. This relationship is central to their identity; it nourishes, strengthens and inspires them all.

This project was the culmination of many years of sharing the Dhurga language across our school and community. We have been fortunate enough to be working in this space since NSW Aboriginal Languages were introduced as part of the school curriculum and have watched the program become an important part of our school. This project will be the first time students from Vincentia High have had the opportunity to share their stories and language with a wider audience. This is an exciting opportunity for our community to showcase the younger generation of Traditional Owners who will continue to carry their language into the future.

Aunty Gai Brown
Aboriginal Education Coordinator

Jonathan Hill
Dhurga Language Teacher
May 2024

marra
bidhanga
baba

gurugama

by Tazza Wellington

djaadjawan between toes.

dhagarr barra barra running through

her fingers.

yuraga milumba bright.

As yuraga glistens against

barra barra,

it rolls up to dhana-dha

Drawn to the beach.

I can hear my name being whispered

in gurugama.

GREEN PATCH

by Elijah Ardler

When the dark patchy shade comes into the
clear barra barra

boys prepare

garawad-bara then walk very calmly

like the dulagaal calm quiet ever so stealthy

marra-waraga stare, all the boys be aware not
to scare!

the boys prepare to marra-waraga

they spear

always be fair and take what you need

always agile

don't be greedy but indeed always feed

a feed

boys cook a feed

it's calm quiet and not even yiribini

waves breaking on shore

always be sure to leave a good feed for dulagaal

otherwise you're gone

bidhu and cliffs shadowing the sea

mungala-waraga covering bunbul-baraga

waves crashing

bunbul-baraga moving

moving ever so slightly

barra barra so calm that marra-waraga are hiding

djaadjawan so white

nothing there to bite

unless you come across wulimbura that will fight you

if you're calm and respectful they won't bite

if you are dumb and fun

you're obviously done!

munggura

by Ruby Butler

Waves crashing against djaadjawan

People screaming in delight

Animals running away from people

The warm yuraga gundhagundha in barra barra

This is what most people call munggura

This is what I call

munggura

GANJi

barra barra bagaranj yiribu-dha

(THE OCEAN AT SUNSET)

by Isabella Van Oploo

barra barra is blue and the waves are calm, barra barra is just singing her song.

The beach is fun when you lay in yuraga.

marra-waraga fly and swim, they also dive in.

The beach is our munggura and the barra barra is our shelter.

But at bagaranj yiribu, the real things come out.

A beautiful life that nobody ever sees.

All controlled by the magical non-human being.

This is the creator that you know as the barra barra with hair like the waves and a beautiful face.

The necklace she wears controls the life of the sea.

But the humans have other plans for her, see?

So if you ever want to free her, listen to me.

Don't you ever throw your trash in the sea.

dhawara

(MOON)

by Allinjah Smith

Take a moment to look at her, Moon
Whether she is waxing, waning or full
She is divine.

dhawara cast biningala over dark lands,
illuminating Country for many to see.

Above, djinggi-waraga dance in her presence,
gadhu sparkles, reaching, calling up to her.

You often remind me of Moon.
You often remind me of dhawara.

Perfection lives in every crevice,
every crater of your soul, and body
It leaves me awestruck.

You project light into my gilwa.
yindiga milumba.

No matter what phase she's in, Moon is mystical.
No matter what phase she's in, we love her.

and in all your fractions and pieces, I love you, my dear.

I love you fully.
I love you boundlessly.

You, like dhawara, are beautiful.

by Alice Ardler

Waves crashing,
all budjan-baraga chirping, screaming.
Nobody here, just Boy and Pop.
Where the shack was,
they are watching the marra-waraga.
barra barra is clear.
Boy and Pop meet in shallow water,
They step slow,
When Boy talks, Pop holds his finger to his own dhaaga.

Ssshhhh

They stretch the net between them,
Drip,
drip,
drip...
One,
two,
three,
Boy and Pop cast their net.

Splash!

Pop grabs the net and pulls,
Boy grabs the net and falls,
All of marra-waraga are trapped.
Boy and Pop take marra-waraga back home
Nan, uncles, aunties, babies – yilaga-waraga is happy
when Boy and Pop

go

to Back Beach.

THE BEACH

by Iesha Walker

I love the beach,
her beautiful blue and white waves,

crashing onto djaadjawan.

She sings a calming sound,

a sound that brings peace to my body and my heart

" W s s h h h h   h h h   h h h   h h h ... "

She sounds better than my beatboxing.

I try to beatbox

it isn't very good.

But that's okay

because I'm at the beach

and the beach is my munggura-dha.

She beatboxes for me.

barra barra-njinungga

OUR OCEAN

by everyone

The peaceful sound of the beautiful blue barra barra, glassy, cool and calm.

biraga bunbal-baraga. Patchy and brown. Spikey, green djirawara. Splotchy gubaa.

njiinj bunbal has a big vine crawling up against it.
Its wulaga is peeling, revealing pale white with brown squiggles.

Cracked, curvy, chipped lines in the wulaga of the log. There's a stringy texture on the back of each stalk connecting to the flower.

It reminds me of a bunbal at home,
perhaps that's why I like it.

The bunbal-baraga are a home for many animals and insects.

There is a budjan looking very curiously at me.
It seems very unbothered. It is smooth to the touch.

barra barra reflects the mirriwarr, mungala-waraga and budjan baraga. It is lighter near the shore, and gets darker further out.

The cold blue barra barra crashes gently against the djaadjawan.

Calm, quiet, and it's not even night. Always be sure to look out for sharks – that's how mob was taught.

5 A.M.

by Tazza Wellington

5 a.m.

The sun is still beneath the earth.

The horizon sleeps peacefully

and birds slip in and out of the sea,

sending ripples across the shore.

Adina lets the weight of her body

sink into the cold sand.

The tide starts to touch her toes

as she hears the birds

sing and

call and

wail.

bilima

by Myles Brown

She is on the edge of her seat waiting for her arrival at Jervis Bay, she is not eager for this day.

She steps out onto the dhagarr djaadjawan as the dharraani tower over her. Feeling the biwaawa wipe straight over her.

She has only ever known ngadju Country, growing up without her mob.

yandabal has always had a part missing from her heart. She has never felt whole.

She can hear her name being whispered in the baliya, calling her towards the barra barra.

As yuraga glistens against barra barra, she watches it roll up to her dhana.

She feels barra barra against her waadhu, strong current starts to draw her out to barra barra.

Panic and fear wash over her as her limbs glide though barra barra like a djungga.

She feels lost and in danger and looks around for help. In the corner of her eye a shell pops up out of the deep blue.

yuraga milumba down on the creatures, it's a bilima.

bilima starts to glow. Her eyes start to run as bilima comforts her.

She realises bilima has come to save her.

The rough, green, sandpaper fin brushes against her mana.

The barra barra runs down her waadhu while the bilima guides her back to shore.

Her body gently drags against the djaadjawan as she cries and cries.

She wipes away her tears. barra barra waadhu-nu-dha.

She knows in her heart bilima is her totem and
she has been barra barra yandabal all along.

MY PEOPLE

by Alice Ardler

Wreck Bay is my munggura-dha,

ngarn where I feel safe.

It's where my mob live.

Wreck Bay is bagan-dha,

where my ancestors rest.

Wreck Bay is my land,

where the beaches are clear

and the waves crash.

Providing marra and seafood for

yuwinj-dha.

barra barra munggura-dha

(THE OCEAN IS MY HOME)

by Pearl Rohrt

salt leaves a cast on my spirally djawur

barra barra wraps around my body, waadhu-dha

messages from bunbal-baraga drift through mirriwarr

patterns on the decaying seashell look almost dotty

animals moving through gadhu, completely free

barra barra munggura-dha

ba njiinj wadha yana-ga

DiViNg

by Jonah Ardler-Pascoe

When I go diving I get

abs, lobsters and marra

I get what I need to feed my family

minga, baaba ba dhadha-waraga-dha

djaadjawan is smooth and soft

wurawura and yellow and calm

As I hit that dark shade of the reef

everything in my mind goes away

fear transforms into motivation

all my senses are alive

before I know it instinct kicks in

ngayaga marra

bardju-mba-ga barra barra-dha.

ngayawanj midandhal bagan-dha

(WE ARE ONE WITH THE LAND)

by Pearl Rohrt

We started our journey by welcoming her. The smoking bunaan connected her with mudjingaal-baraga ba bagan.

duruuwa weaved through her hair. ngayawanj midandhal bagan-dha.

I taught her the importance of the mamaadja and that it is needed for the bunaan. Its nutrient-filled djirawara create a dampness that welcomes the ancestors.

We watched the white curls of duruuwa form and waited for our turn. ngayawanj midandhal bagan-dha.

After connecting she learned the cultural roles of the animals. gari, djagula ba bilima. She also learnt about business for gimbanya-waraga and ngaranggal-baraga through the garawad dance.

Everyone stomped their feet on bagan, rising the dust, awakening and joining muladha-waraga ba gamara-waraga.

bunaan connected us all. ngayawanj midandhal bagan-dha.

She learnt about yuwinj-nu. The connection is strong mamaadja-dha, bunaan-dha, duruuwa-dha, bilima-dha.

ngayawanj midandhal bagan-dha.

ngayawanj bagan-nggul

by Jonathan Hill

ngayawanj bagan-nggul

ngayawanj njiinj bagan-nggul

ngayawanj barra barra-nggul

ngayawanj bunbal-baraga-nggul gadhu-dha

yuraga dhalibawa-n mirriwarr-dha

milumba mungala-waraga, gundhagundha

mina-waraga duruuwa ganji-din

mina-waraga yuraga, bagaranj, dhawara

maya-nj djaadjawan-dha ganji-dha. dhumbama-nj
duruuwa. dhumbama-nj mirriwarr.

yuraga, dhawara, baliya barra barra-dha

maya-nj. djanbabu-nj. dhumbama-nj mirriwarr

milumba mungala-waraga, gundhagundha

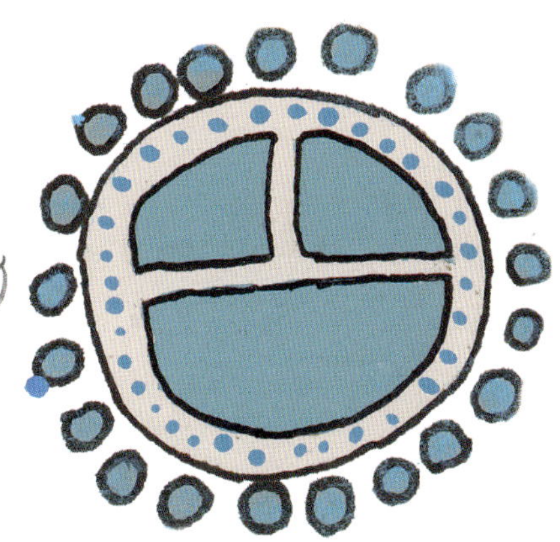

WE BELONG TO THE LAND

we belong to the land

we belong to this land

we belong to the sea

we belong to these trees by the ocean

the sun goes up to the sky

shining clouds, sparkling

they hold the smoke from the fire

they hold the sun, the heat, the moon

we sit on the sand by the fire. we look at the smoke.
we look at the sky.

the sun, the moon, the north east wind on the sea

we sit. we are silent. we look at the sky.

shining clouds, sparkling.

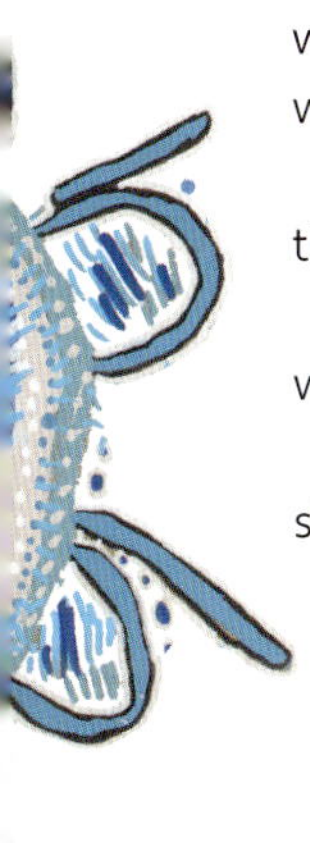

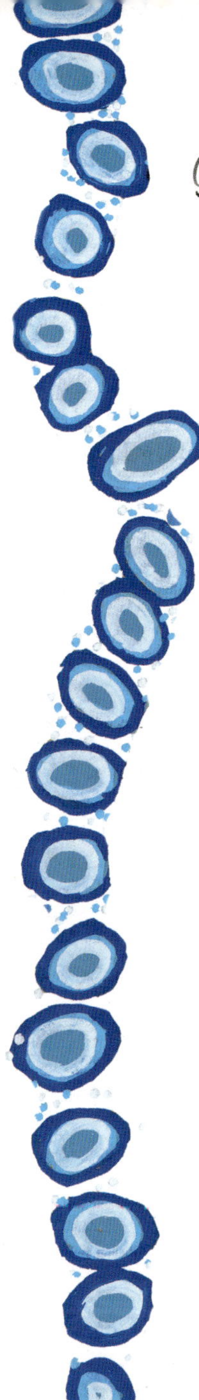

GLOSSARY

ba	and
baaba	dad
bagan	earth
bagaranj yiribu	sunset
baliya	northeast wind
bardju-mba-ga	I am swimming
barra barra	ocean
barra barra-dha	in the sea
barra barra yandabal	saltwater girl
bidhu	mountains
bilima	turtle
binin.gala	light, moonlight, sunlight
biraga	large
biwaawa	cold east wind
budjan	bird
bunbal	tree
buru	kangaroo
dhaaga	mouth
dhadha-waraga-dha	my brothers
dhagarr	cold
dhana	feet
dharraani	spotted gum
dhawara	moon
djaadjawan	sand
djagula	lyrebird
djawur	hair
djinggi	star
djirawara	leaves
djungga	octopus
dulagaal	hairy man
duruuwa	smoke
gadhu	rough sea
garawad	fishing spear
garawad-bara	two spears
gari	snake
gilwa	darkness

Glossary (cont.)

gimbanya-waraga	men
gubaa	stringy bark
gundhagundha	sparkling
gurugama	west wind
mamaadja	native cherry
marra	fish
marida	sea eagle
milumba	shine
minga	mum
mirriwarr	sky
mudjingaal-baraga	spirit protectors
mungala-waraga	clouds
munggura	home
ngadju	fresh water
ngaranggal-baraga	women
ngarn	a place
ngayaga	I am
ngayawanj midandhal bagan-dha	we are one with the land
njiinj	this
wadha	where
waadhu	skin
wulaga	bark
wulimbura	shark
wurawura	white
yana-ga	I go
yandabal	girl
yilaga-waraga	everyone is happy
yindiga	you
yiribini	night
yuraga	sun
yuwinj-dha	my Yuin People

Suffixes

-baraga (used after a consonant)	many
-dha	my
-dha	on, at, by, with
-waraga (used after a vowel)	many

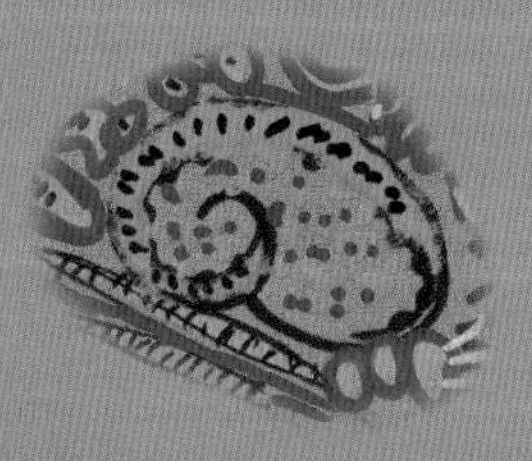

Acknowledgements

The Ganya Garindja Aboriginal Education Team, comprising Aunty Gai Brown, Aunty Jannine Brown, Jonathan Hill, Bri McLeod-Cosgrove and Taylor-Lee Byrne would like to thank the following people who have been instrumental in our Dhurga Language revitalisation journey:

Aunty Glad Worthy and Gary Worthy, for their role in establishing the Dhurga Language Program at Vincentia High and for their ongoing support and advocacy.

Karen Lane, for her commitment to teaching Dhurga for over a decade in conjunction with local community members and for her overall contribution to Aboriginal Education at Vincentia High.

Wreck Bay Community for their cultural wisdom, guidance and custodianship.

George Brown, for being a staunch advocate for our kids and programs and for allowing us the chance to undertake this project at the magnificent Green Patch Beach in Booderee National Park.

Ruth Winfield, for your leadership, enduring support and high expectations that you have for all our kids.

Aunty Patricia Ellis, Aunty Kerry Boyenga and Uncle Waine Donovan, your dictionary has been an invaluable resource that continues to shape, transform and inspire entire communities throughout the Yuin Nation.

Jaz Corr, for the beautiful way you brought the students and community together to create two truly collaborative artworks that perfectly reflect the strength of our connection to the land and sea.

Kirli Saunders, for the magical workshops you conducted which allowed creativity to flow.

Marion Worthy, for your help and support, not only during the workshops but with resources and cultural guidance in the delivery of the Dhurga program.

Elizabeth Arrigo, Jolene Brown, Ella Schofield and Emma Toomey – thank you for coordinating the workshops and allowing the time to flow seamlessly from one activity to the next. The kids are still talking about the chicken-salted chip sandwiches!

Elizabeth Arrigo – a massive thank you to you for bringing it all together and not only giving our students the chance to engage on a deeper level with their culture, but giving them a platform to share their experience with the world.

Nigel Marsden, you sparked the fire which brought this whole project to life.

About the Indigenous Literacy Foundation

The Indigenous Literacy Foundation (ILF) is a national charity working with Aboriginal and Torres Strait Islander remote Communities across Australia. We are Community-led, responding to requests from remote Communities for culturally relevant books, including early learning board books, resources, and programs to support Communities to create and publish their stories in languages of their choice.

First published in 2024 by the Indigenous Literacy Foundation
Level 17, 207 Kent Street
Sydney NSW 2000
ilf.org.au

This project supported by The PNI Foundation / Five V Capital

Cataloguing-in-Publication details are available from the National Library of Australia
www.trove.nla.gov.au

9781922592781

Typesetting and design by Justine Taylor
Printed by RR Donnelley Asia Printing Solutions Limited